THE PARTY, OI

LED TO ANOTHER

All characters, apart from the obvious historical figures, in this publication are fictitious and any resemblance to real persons, alive or dead, is purely coincidental.

Copyright © Richard Giles 2022

IF YOU ENJOY READING THIS SHORT STORY, OR IF YOU LIKE MY QUIRKY STYLE OF WRITING AND HUMOUR, THEN WHY NOT READ MY OTHER BOOKS?

SO FAR, I HAVE PUBLISHED TWO, AS PART OF A TWO-PART SERIES. THAT SERIES IS A HISTORICAL COMICAL DRAMA, COVERING THE YEARS 1064-1066, ABOUT A STRONG-WILLED AND POWERFUL WOMAN, DUCHESS MATILDA OF NORMANDY, WHO WILL STOP AT NOTHING TO ENSURE HER HUSBAND, WILLIAM, DUKE OF NORMANDY, BECOMES KING OF ENGLAND. YOU DON'T NEED TO LIKE HISTORY TO ENJOY IT!

THE PARTY, OR ONE THING LED TO ANOTHER

6: 15 P.M.

Charles sighed as he looked at himself in the mirror. As usual, he was not looking forward to one of his wife's drinks parties. It usually went badly for him. He always started with good intentions, but events tended to get out of hand. *Thinking about it,* he thought, *there were really just two events in the evening that were pleasant, one at the beginning and one at the end.* Anne, his wife, was fussing as usual. She liked to plan everything down to the last crisp. He knew he was on her list, and was currently checking whether he would pass inspection. He loved her dearly but…. He sighed again.

As he looked in the mirror, he thought, *I don't look bad for a man of 30!* Luckily the war had treated him quite well. He had been an RAF fighter pilot stationed at Biggin Hill, south of London. He was only 21 when the air war known by the British as the Battle of Britain commenced. It had really started in late August 1940, and that was when he joined his Spitfire squadron. He had been thrown into the war as a novice with only 15 hours flying time in a spitfire. He was going to be lucky to survive days let alone the war, but survive he did. He quickly learnt the tactics and skills to stay alive against a much more experienced foe in a much more potent fighter, the ME109. Once he could survive being shot down, it took him another three weeks before he hit an enemy with his machine guns. After that it seemed easy, the main risks were tiredness, bad judgment, drink, or sheer bad luck. He soon became an ace and national hero. All that was behind him. He looked in the mirror again and sighed.

'Those were the days he whispered,' then he laughed, 'you chump those days were hell on earth.'

Anne shouted from the kitchen, 'What are you laughing at?'

'Nothing, dear!'

He looked in the mirror and sighed, whispering, 'I just can't fail inspection this time as she's sure to take it as a deliberate act designed to upset her.'

Another shout came from the kitchen, along with the clatter of bone china, 'Dear, you're not talking to that over-weight cat of yours again?'

'At least he understands me,' he whispered.

Charles was wearing a nice crisply ironed pale blue shirt, open at the collar accompanied by a dark blue cravat, his check jacket, black trousers, RAF socks and black shoes. *Thank God,* he thought, *that she no longer insists on me having to wear a dinner suit and bow tie.* He said to himself, 'Charlie Bishop, life is passing you by!'

In the mirror he could see his medals displayed above the fire place. He was not sure whether he liked to be reminded of them and what they really represented, him as a hero, or as a killer. He could no longer rejoice in having killed other human beings, even though they were Nazis. Anne, however had other ideas, and had them put on display. She was proud of them and the social standing they gave.

Anne breezed into the lounge. She was nearly as beautiful as she had been when he first met her. With her blond hair, blue eyes, and body that went in and out in all the right places, she was still quite a stunner. Perhaps a little overweight though. He thought further, *yes probably a result of all those parish council and church meetings. Those homemade cakes and scones can do havoc to a woman's figure.*

'Ah, darling, let me see, yes very dashing, um, are you sure about those socks?'

She gave him another look from top to toe and added, 'You'll do, I suppose.'

She breezed out, followed by Charles shouting, 'I'll change my socks then.'

He sat down and lit a cigarette. He never used to smoke, but during the war they handed them out like sweets, part of a service man's rations. He inhaled deeply and tried to relax. *Well,* he thought, *I think I passed parade. I know what, I'll rebel and leave the blasted socks on!* He inhaled again. He tried to think back to when he first met her and started going out with her. She had certainly changed. Not only was she a lot more religious, especially in the last five years, but she was also oh so well organized. *Yes,* he thought, *she has matured a hell of a lot more than I have!*

It all started on December 15, 1941. He and his best friend and fellow officer, William, best known as Bill or Billy Boy, were sitting in the Lyon's Corner House on Tottenham Court Road, when two of the most

5

beautiful women either had ever laid eyes on walked in. They were surely identical twins, and both as equally angelic-like in appearance, and the way they walked, well it was pure poetry in motion. They too were wearing RAF uniforms, and appeared to look their way, whispered to each other and nodded, and then sat themselves down at the next table. They pretended to study the menu, but the boys could see that their interest was elsewhere.

Eventually one of them tapped Bill on the shoulder. 'Are you that Wing Commander Charles Bishop, DFC and so forth?'

Bill was too shy to say anything, so just pointed his finger at Charles.

Charles laughed again, and thought, *yes, and that was that, one thing led to another and soon their lives would be changed forever.*

There was a voice from the kitchen, 'Is that you laughing again?'

'No dear, it's the cat, I'm tickling his stomach.' He said to his constant companion, 'Winston, it seems I'm not allowed to laugh now! I think I'm on a charge!'

Winston just looked at Charles, and replied, 'Meow!' thinking, *I love my non-cat servant, but he could feed me more often!* The cat decided to be more vocal, 'Meow, meow, meooow!'

Charles laughed and shook his head at Winston. 'Well, Winnie, a very harsh observation, but correct as usual!'

Anne put her head around the kitchen door. 'Well, if you've nothing better to do but lark about with that flea-bitten monster, then you could help me by getting the drinks bottles, cocktail shaker, and glasses sorted.'

Anne went back to the kitchen to give the help their orders for the night.

Charles sighed. He knew a sergeant major like Anne. *Yes, Sally and Anne were great company, and both Billy Boy and myself were, I think, equally smitten. But we could not decide which would be the better wife,* Charles laughed, *so one day we went to our local pub near the airfield, and whilst sitting at our usual table, drinking warm beer from our usual tankards, tried to resolve matters.*

The same voice from the kitchen interrupted, 'Is that smoke I can smell, I hope you are not getting ash over those newly polished tables and cleaned carpet.'

Charles studied the end of his cigarette and tapped the end so the ash drifted down on the side table and carpet.

'No dear, it's the cat, he's on fire.'

His thoughts continued, *it took all night, and six pints each, but in the end, we put their two names in my cap, and Bill drew one of the two pieces of paper. And the rest is history as they say, one thing led to another, and Bill married Sally and I married Anne. Neither of us have had any children. Anne did not want any, and as regards Sally and Bill, well, Anne told me that was due to some sort of medical issue. Still, up until poor Bill's accident 5 years ago, they had been constant companions. Now it's just me, Anne, and Winston, and of course her crazy sister Sally.*

Right, he thought, *smoke break over, I'd better get the booze and glasses organized.* 'Where's the ice darling?'

Anne sighed and then shouted, 'In the freezer where else would it be?'

Charles shrugged his shoulders. 'In the cat?' and trudged into the kitchen, followed by a tabby fury cannon ball hoping for something tasty.

7: 15 P.M.

'Listen to me carefully Charles, before the guests arrive, remember I don't want any repeat of what happened at the last party, and several of those before.'

Charles replied calmly, 'It's not always my fault, its your—'

Anne interjected before he had time to finish, 'Yes, I know, but please try for my sake. Be nice for a change.'

Charles grumbled, 'I'll try but it won't make any difference.'

He couldn't think what else to say so walked out onto the terrace. It was a lovely moon-lit early evening in April. There was still the red and orange glow in the sky to the west left by the recently set sun, and a full moon rising in the east. *It would be a very romantic sky tonight and that's a fact,* he thought, *but knowing the guest list, I think Frank Beesley was going to be the best-looking guest but definitely the wrong gender. But if I get this Friday evening out of the way, I could perhaps sneak off for a round of golf tomorrow with my old flying chums.*

Golf had become a regular Saturday thing, and Anne no longer complained about it. To begin with she said it was anti-social, in other words, not fair on her, but over the last five years, she seemed not to complain, or just to complain for the sake of it. It was as if she didn't care any more one way or the other.

She had her life, and he had some of his life, and some of hers.

7: 35 P.M.

All the guests had arrived except one, the usual one. Charles had personally prepared and served drinks to all. He liked that duty. *Not only do I get to have a crafty drink or two, well I have to make sure that the cocktails are just right, don't I?* But he also got to meet Anne's friends with minimal contact. He always had the excuse of having to make more refreshments and he could never be accused of not circulating nor of being anti-social. The throng had now gravitated into three main topics of conversation. There was the knotty problem as to how to eradicate earwigs infesting your Dahlias. The men had huddled together in the corner by the piano and were, as usual, starting with the safe topic of conversation, motorcars. Finally, Anne was holding court, centre stage, and that group was tackling the morality of obtaining black market or off-ration book provisions. Charles laughed to himself, thinking, *well, Anne will be on a sticky wicket there, given the ingredients of the buffet tonight, let alone the booze.*

There was a knock on the door, it was THAT knock, dot, dash, dashy, dash, dash, dot. He sighed, then opened the door.

Immediately Sally started on the attack. 'Hello, Charlie Boy, looking peaky I see, she who must be obeyed not feeding you properly? Well just don't stand there like a startled haddock, take my coat, I'm in the mood for some mischief!'

Charles obliged, revealing the body of a goddess in a light blue dress matching the colour of her eyes. It was a definite "Sally" dress, daring and just about socially acceptable. 'Please don't call me Charlie Boy, I'm not a race horse!' He hated the way she said his name and he knew that she knew too. However, he liked the way she looked, and he knew that she knew it too as well.

Charles dropped Sally's coat on the chair in the hall, startling the cat that had been sleeping there. The cat waddled off outside in disgust after clawing the offending garment.

Charles took his gaze off the cat, thinking, *well done Winston!* and turned towards Sally, saying, 'Hello you, late as usual.'

She laughed and replied, 'Not rudely late, just fashionably late.'

Charles could only think of replying, 'If you say so.'

She laughed again. 'I do, and nice shirt by the way, but shame about those socks. Jumble sale presumably?'

Charles grimaced, thinking, *she always had to have the last word, and why was she always so jolly? What's she got to be jolly about in any case?* Charles was now studying her dress, *a simple but effective weapon,* he thought, *although the neckline does seem a touch too revealing!*

She continued on the attack. 'Well, Charles dear, don't wear your eyes out, and sorry I'm late, but you know what they say, a flawless diamond is worth waiting for.'

Charles was not very good at this verbal game; he knew she was in a class of her own. Anne had heard her sister's last sentence and came over and greeted Sally.

She kissed her sister on both cheeks. 'Lovely to see you, glad you could eventually make it. Lovely dress, dear, but perhaps a touch audacious. Still, I suppose it depends what sort of impression you wish to make.'

Sally looked her sister up and down. 'Nice tweed suit, sister darling, you must be sweltering in such a tight thing. Perhaps that would be fine if you were going duck shooting in the park. Oh, sister dear, have you put on weight? Perhaps Charles is not keeping you fully exercised.'

Anne sighed. 'Drink, dear? Where's Charles?'

They both looked round, Sally shrugged her shoulders. 'I must have scared him off.'

Then they saw him approaching them from the direction of the dining room holding a chair.

'Darling, what are you doing?' Anne enquired.

'I'm sitting here on this chair until that flawless diamond of hers appears.'

'Ha Ha HA,' shouted Sally, 'very funny I don't think.'

Anne chastised Charles. 'Don't be stupid Charles, make Sally a drink, and remember what you promised.'

Sally laughed. 'Yes, do what you're told, make me a drink.'

Charles grumbled as he started to take the chair back to the dining room.

Anne commanded, 'Stop, and greet your sister-in-law properly, and do it in a polite fashion!'

Charles grumbled again, putting the chair down. He put his hands on Sally's bare upper arms, and kissed her on both cheeks. A hot tingling sensation, starting from his face and ending in his groin, purveyed his whole body. His face went crimson.

Both women noticed, but Sally was the first to comment, 'Been at the booze again? You know it's no good for you. Now talking of drinks, where's mine?'

She brushed past Charles and headed for the small bar in the lounge, she was feeling very flushed, a shiver had gone right through her body, ending up in her toes. In no way was she going to show it, so she headed for the cool of the terrace.

Charles followed with the chair, for some reason he took it for a walk all the way to the terrace.

'Are you stalking me?' asked Sally, lighting a cigarette.

Charles ignored this accusation and retorted, 'Have you been drinking?'

Sally suddenly had a tear or three in her eyes, and they dropped down her soft pink cheeks, and ended up on her chin. 'You louse, yes, I've had a drink, I needed it today of all days! Don't you remember, that terrible day was precisely 5 years ago!'

Charles was still studying her face, and was not fully concentrating. '5 Years since what?'

Sally was not amused. 'You, You, insensitive pig. 5 years since the death of—'

Charles leaped forward and gave her a hug. 'Oh, I'm sorry, forgive me, I was distracted by, um, your dress.'

Sally was quite happy with his embrace, but felt she needed to make a point. She disconnected and slapped his face. Charles was startled but regained his composure, thinking he deserved that. All he could think of saying was, 'Drink?'

'Oh, yes I'll have a—'

Charles interrupted, 'Good choice, I'll get two weak ones.' And off he trotted, leaving his new wooden four-legged best friend for Sally to sit on.

Sally was wishing that she had a fan, like those women in the old days who would swoon all over the place whilst heaving their bosoms at the slightest glance from their admirers. Charles returned with two dry martinis, both with black and green olives, stirred not shaken.

Sally sipped hers. 'Lovely. You're certainly good at one thing.'

He moved to the railing and stared at the moon, it was full and bright, and the reflection off the pond beyond the terrace was amazing.

Sally got to her feet and stood next to him, but not too close. 'A lovely night.'

Charles turned and looked at her in the moonlight. It was all too much. 'Sally—'

Sally interrupted. 'Yes, I know, good idea, perhaps we should indeed mingle.'

She moved gracefully into the lounge, leaving Charles, his chair, and his moon alone together. He sighed and followed.

8: 10 P.M.

Sally joined a group discussing baking. Charles joined the men talking about their cars. He was an expert since he currently worked as a salesman in an up-market car show room in Mayfair. When that debate ended, he replenished people's drinks. As he held the tray of cocktails, he sipped his. He thought, *so far so good! I actually think that tonight will go very smoothly indeed! Role on tomorrow and the golf!*

His last port of call was the baking group. They were discussing how to get bread to rise nicely. He was just in time; Sally was starting to make some strange comments when he arrived, finishing with, 'What ingredients could be added to make, say, a man to rise, perhaps a little lacy number but do you fin—?'

Charles grabbed her by the right shoulder and pulled her away. He shook his head laughing softly. 'Sally please don't.'

'Well, rising bread, whatever next!'

Charles offered her a drink from the tray, 'Another drink?'

'Yes please, but I'll have a—'

'Good idea, I'll join you in one of those.'

He returned within a couple of minutes, with two black Russians.

'Ah, just what the doctor ordered, oh, talking about doctors, do you remember that day 5 years ago?'

They sipped their drinks, remembering that morning with the doctor.

Sally turned to Charles. 'Charlie, you know how I—'

The sentence was cut short by a Mrs Katie Neugent, the new vice chairman of the Parish Council. 'Ah, Wing Commander, it's an honour to meet you at last! You're such a brave man. You must have many stories to tell, and all those medals.' She pointed at the display case and smiled broadly.

Charles remaining polite, replied kindly and modestly to Mrs Neugent, 'Oh, it was nothing.'

Sally was livid with the woman as she had spoilt the moment.

Mrs Neugent was persistent. 'Please do show them to me.'

'Of course, I'll get them.'

Sally grumbled under her breath, 'Stupid woman! I nearly told Charlie! Why doesn't she go and discuss her huge dumplings? They're certainly big enough!'

Some of the rest of the guests saw Charles get the case, and came over to have a closer look. There was now a large circle. Sally emptied her glass, and studied the emptiness of its inside; it reminded her of her own life.

Charles pointed. 'Well, this is the DFC, and this is my favourite, the VC, presented to me by no less than the late King.'

There was a collective, 'OOH.'

Sally was first to speak, 'Why is the king so late these days, that's what I want to know!'

Charles kicked her lightly on the right shin.

'Owe that hurt.'

Everyone turned towards Sally.

Charles rushed in first. 'Sorry dear, my foot slipped. Well, and here in this drawer is the letter from Winston Churchill praising me about that mission—'

General Hardcore was in awe. 'Yes, bally good show that, and all hush hush at the time, and behind German lines to boot.'

Mrs Neugent was entranced, and smitten. 'And how many planes did you shoot down, Wing Commander?'

'Oh, 21 confirmed and several unconfirmed, and a few half kills.'

Sally had had enough. 'And which half of the plane did you kill then? Did the other half escape to fight another day?'

The general coughed. 'Well, I say jolly good show, what.'

Sally was off again. 'Quite frankly, I think that anyone who goes about gloating and boasting about killing humans, are a bit, well, insensitive and immature if not dim-witted!'

Charles went red, but now for a different reason. 'I was not gloating. I was merely—'

'Yes, telling us how you murdered young men.'

The general sprang to Charles's defence. 'They were Nazis and they started it first.'

Sally replied vehemently, wagging her finger at the General, 'Killing is killing and it's a sin.'

The group were becoming uneasy, and started drifting away, eventually leaving just Sally and an embarrassed Charles. Charles slipped his medals in a drawer in his desk. For some reason they were making him feel uncomfortable. For the first time, he was feeling less than the hero people thought he was.

He returned to Sally. 'Drink?'

'Good idea. I'll have a—'

'Yes, perfect,' and off he trotted.

He soon returned with two Brandy Alexanders.

She looked at the drink intently. 'How did you know?'

'I always do.'

Sally nodded and sighed, saying, 'Yes, I understand.'

Charles put his hand on her bare shoulder. 'No, I'm not clairvoyant, it's just that you are predicable.'

Sally laughed, and held his free hand. 'You've noticed?'

Charles was starting to feel hot again. 'Of course.'

'Yes Charlie, of course. Oh, Charlie?'

'Yes, Sally, that's me.'

Sally looked like she was about to cry. 'I'm sorry.'

Charles was astounded, it was the first time in the last five years or so that she had said that. Charles looked at Sally closely, and went to kiss her. 'Dearest Sally—'

They were interrupted by Anne. 'Well, you two, congratulations, you've already managed to upset half my guests. There's half to go, behave and circulate, one of you circulate clockwise and one circulate anti-clockwise.'

Being the best policy in the circumstances, both obeyed, Charles went to the men who were now discussing golf, another safe topic.

Sally moved through one group that included Father O'Neil. 'Yes, I was late tonight because of a crisis of faith of one of—'

Sally butted in, 'Oh, we all lose our faith in God, Father, but don't worry, just go and see a priest about it, unless you want to talk to me, I'm understanding and a great listener.'

With that passing remark she immediately moved on and joined a group discussing fashion, a topic she could certainly enjoy and contribute constructively to, leaving the priest trying to explain that it was not his crisis of faith but that of one of his parishioners.

Eventually, the men got on to stocks and shares, and the women onto jam making. Charles and Sally ended up together near the piano, since neither topic were of interest.

Charles pointed to her empty glass. 'Another drink?'

'Why not.'

Charles returned with two large tonic waters.

Sally took a sip and grimaced, but then smiled. 'You're right, I think it's going to be a long evening.'

Both looked longingly at the terrace.

Sally was first. 'Shall we?'

Charles shook his head. 'Better not.'

They looked at each other.

Charles was the first to speak, 'Strange night tonight, I have a good feeling that we may remain civilized for a change. Sally, I—'

'Yes, I know Charles.'

'When?'

'That day at Brighton, Charlie.'

Charles nodded. 'Yes, Bill and Anne had gone off to see the Brighton Pavilion.'

Sally laughed, 'Yes, they were always interested in culture. I remember we sat on the hotel's terrace in the afternoon sun, drinking martinis, chatting about this and that, and finding we had so much in common, and then when—'

Charles interrupted. 'Yes.' Charles laughed. 'When they returned, we were both legless. They ordered afternoon tea, we ordered strong coffee, and stayed sitting in our chairs until we could feel our feet again!'

'I don't think they noticed,' Sally replied, laughing.

Charles looked at Sally. 'Sally—'

He felt for her hand, they touched again.

Anne noticed, and walked over. 'Lovely to see you getting on for a change, and you've only upset half the guests, well done!'

9: 05 P.M.

Anne looked towards the open patio doors, 'Lovely night out there, if you two want some fresh air, now's the time, and you both look a bit flustered. It's candlelight buffet time soon.'
    Anne walked back to Mrs Neugent with a smile on her face.
    Charles looked at Sally. 'Shall we?'
    Sally shook her head. 'No, too—'
    'Yes, you're right, definitely too. I'm sure one thing would surely lead to another!'
    They continued looking deeply into each other's eyes. Charles was first to break free.
    He coughed. 'Another drink?'
    'Yes, Charlie, but—'
    'You're right, Sal, perhaps—'
    'Yes, I agree, Charlie, it's time to stop these—'
    'Urges, Sally dear?'
    Sally nodded.
    Charles left Sally on her own; Anne glanced over and smiled at her sister. That unnerved Sally more than any words. *She knows!*
    Charles returned with two more tonics.
    Sally whispered to Charles, 'Anne knows!'
    Charles nearly spilt the drinks as he turned and looked for Anne.
    Anne looked at him and smiled.

Charles shook his head. 'No, surely not. If she did, I'd get a rolling pin smashed across my head not a smile!'

They both took sips and gazed at the enticing terrace. Sally shivered. 'You know I hate tonic on its own!'

Charles agreed and said, 'Me too, it's like drinking liver salts!'

Sally nodded and agreed. 'But then—'

Charles laughed. 'Yes, we must do penance and this stuff certainly brings me back to earth.' Sally nodded again, grimaced, and took another gulp of her medicine. They walked over to the piano.

'Do you play, or is it just for show?' Sally enquired.

'I play but not to an audience. I used to be a music student until the Nazis interrupted, and I still practice when Anne is away at one of her blasted charity meetings.'

Sally was intrigued, she never knew. 'I didn't know Charlie, play something.'

'Well, if you insist, but I've never played in front of Anne let alone anyone else.'

'Play something just for me, Charlie dear.'

Charles looked at Anne but she was deep in conversation. *She's not going to like this*, he thought, *but here goes nothing.* He gulped down the rest of the tonic, shivered, and sat down at the piano. What followed could only be described as a sensation. He started with his favourite piece, which he thought apt given the sky that could be viewed from the terrace, Debussy's Clair de Lune. Everyone stopped talking, and listened, afterwards all agreed that it had been one of the best interpretations that they ever had heard. Sally rested her right hand on Charles's left shoulder as he played. She was very moved with his playing, somehow it made her tearful, and thoughts drifted back to when they first met, and her last days with her husband, William, and other sad memories, and those guilty secrets. At the end of the piece, there was loud applause.

Mrs Katie Neugent, having already succumbed to Charles's charms, could not contain herself. 'Anne, dear, you never told me you had not only married a hero, but a piano virtuoso as well!'

Anne was stunned but recovered her composure. 'He's so modest about it.'

Mrs Neugent clapped all the way over to the piano and asked, 'Wing Commander, play some more, please.'

Charles smiled at her. 'Call me Charles.'

He looked at Sally and then at Anne. They both nodded. He had a think, *the last piece had got me a scholarship at music college, I know,* he thought. Keeping the theme romantic, he played Bach's Moonlight Sonata, first movement. Again, the room went quiet. Charles looked at Sally as he played. She knew only too well its relevance. So did Anne.

After another rapturous applause, Anne put up her right hand. 'After that wonderful music, food for the soul as they say, what could be more apt than some refreshments under the moon and stars.'

9: 45 P M

The guests walked purposefully, but with an air of dignity.

Anne came over to Charles and Sally who were the only other people left in the lounge. 'Just in case, best you both stay here, I don't want a repeat of what happened last time when you, Charles ended up with trifle in your hair, and you, Sally received the contents of a fruit salad bowl in retaliation. And, as for you, Charles, I must say, well done, but we must have no secrets you know.' She looked both of them in the eyes. 'No secrets!' and off she went to join her guests.

Her maid, Joan had laid everything out splendidly, and she and her younger cousin, Daisy, were serving the hungry guests.

The General was still having a debate about the music. 'It's all well and good in its own way, but I like a tune that a chap can march to.'

Mrs Neugent nodded. 'Yes, but the Wing Commander has a deep soul, I can tell.'

'Well yes, I suppose, but that type of music will never win wars, why when I was in India I,' the General stopped talking whilst he finished off a scotch egg that was failing to surrender without a fight, and then continued his monologue, 'used to....'

His speech continued.

Meanwhile Sally looked at Charles. 'Charles, Anne does know.'

Charles choked on his bitter lemon slice. 'Anne knows what exactly?'

'Anne knows about us.'

Charles shook his head, asking, 'What about us? We haven't done anything.'

'Well not in a physical way.'

Charles looked gloomily at the remains of the lemon. 'Yes, you're right. Another drink?'

'Please, but not another tonic! I know just for a change, like we did in the old days, get us both a long but weak—'

'Yes, perfect in the circumstances, not had one for over 5 years. I think the last one we had was when William was still, oh, well, I'll get us one each then!'

It took a while, but Charles came back with two Wicked Temptations, one of his own concoctions. The four of them used to enjoy them in the old days. She joined him on the piano stool. 'Charlie dear, play something else, please.'

'I don't think that's a good idea. I know what's next, and it's more romantic than the other two, and as they say, one thing can lead to another.'

He turned round and faced her, and she did likewise, he took both her hands in his. 'Sally I lov—'

Sally put her finger on his lips. 'Sh, I know.'

They were just about to embrace, when the General marched in. 'Now look here, Bishop, Katie Neugent says you've got too much soul or some such balderdash, but you being a military man must be able to play proper band music. Oh, sorry did I interrupt something?'

Charles let go of Sally's hands. 'What would you like sir, something with a bit of umpf?'

'Precisely.'

Charles started to play the British Grenadiers March.

'Yes, that's it, that's it!'

The General smiled, whistled and then went back for his dessert.

'You see Katie, he's not the arti farti type. I tell you this, if I had any of those in my regiment, I got them peeling potatoes pronto. Nothing like peeling spuds to eradicate any of that type of behaviour. Now when I was in India…' The monologue continued on the terrace.

Charles turned to Sally. 'Now where were we?'

'Just about to need another tonic water I think.'

'Yes, you're right.'

Sally sighed, looking at the black piano keys. 'Yes.'

Charles stopped the march, and started playing Chopin's Nocturne in e flat. 'Another drink?'

Sally shook her head. 'No thanks I'll just sit here.'

After a while she continued. 'Charles please stop and listen.'

'Alrighty.' and he closed the lid of the piano.

Sally looked into his face. 'Charles, Anne—'

Mrs Neugent burst in. 'Don't stop Wing Com, I mean Charles, that was lovely, oh, sorry was I interrupting something, I'm often accused of that. And remember, call me Katie!'

'Not at all, Mrs, I mean Katie, I'm just giving my fingers a rest.'

'Then promise me that you will play some more later.'

'I promise, Katie.'

Mrs Neugent practically danced back onto the terrace thinking, he called me Katie.

Charles turned to Sally. 'Now where were we?'

Sally tried again. 'Charles, Anne never wanted children, did she?'

Charles sighed, 'No.'

'Did she ever explain why?'

'She said her life was full enough looking after me, and then there was all the charity and community work she did. She also confided to me that she just didn't like the thought of it.'

Sally couldn't help herself be a bit flippant. 'What the conception or the birth?'

Charles sort of squirmed on the piano stool and looking down at his feet and twiddling the embroidered cover that was on the stool replied, 'Well, quite frankly and truthfully, I think both.'

Sally could not stop herself from laughing. 'Poor dear boy.'

Charles was feeling very uncomfortable and Sally knew it. 'Oh, sorry, I'm so sorry!' and she bent over and kissed him on the forehead.

He raised his head towards hers. 'Sally, I—'

Father O'Neil entered the room. 'Oh, sorry you two, am I interrupting? It's just that I need to use the phone. The elderly father of one of my parishioners is very ill. He was hit by a train earlier today.'

Charles tried to sound concerned. 'Oh really, it's serious then?'

The priest nodded. 'Of course, trains are pretty heavy you know.'

Charles continued. 'Where was he hurt?'

'On his head.'

Charles laughed, 'No, I mean where did this take place, at the station or somewhere on the railway line?'

Father O'Neil shook his head. 'Neither, in his dining room.'

Charles was amazed. 'Gosh the train derailed into his house, talk about unlucky.'

Father O'Neil shook his head. 'It was his grandson's fault.'

Sally giggled, saying, 'Why was he driving the train?'

Sally chuckled again.

Father O'Neil shook his head again. 'No, Mrs Brown, don't be so silly! His grandson hit him over the head with a Hornby model train made of sharp and heavy metal.'

Sally giggled, and said, 'I'm sure he had a good reason.'

The priest shrugged. 'I suppose, you see it was the lad's birthday, and he wanted roller skates not a train set. He didn't appreciate the present that's for sure!'

Charles had had enough of this silly conversation. He pointed to the hall. 'It's on the hall table.'

Sally couldn't let go. 'What the train?' and giggled again.

Charles looked sharply at her. 'No, you desirable idiot, the telephone you ass!'

Father O'Neil walked off, thinking, *that's no way to talk in the presence of a man of the cloth.*

29

Charles turned to Sally. 'Right, as I was sayi—'

Frank Beesley walked into the room. 'Do you know where the little room is? I'm a martyr to my bladder, and it's playing up all of a sudden, I think it was that curried egg. Oh, sorry am I interrupting?'

Charles pointed to the door opposite. 'Second on the left.'

Frank walked slowly off, keeping his legs together and trying not to leak on the carpet.

Charles looked at Sally. 'Now where were we?'

Miss Trout ambled in. 'Anyone seen Frank, I have saved him some trifle. Oh, sorry am I interrupting you two?'

Sally screamed in frustration. A startled Miss Trout jumped. Charles for once thought quickly, especially given the cocktail of drinks in his stomach. 'Sorry, I just stepped on Mrs Brown's foot.'

Miss Trout, the ever practical, responded concerned, 'I'll get some ice, where's the kitchen?'

Charles sighed. 'Through the door opposite, first on the left, in the kitchen, in the freezer and not the oven! If you miss that door, you'll be with Frank in the toilet.'

Miss Trout left, task in hand.

Charles looked at Sally. 'At last, where were we?'

'Up the Amazon without a paddle.'

The rest of the guests drifted in, joined by Frank with his empty bladder, and Miss Trout with the ice.

Mrs Neugent made a beeline for Charles. 'Please play something.'

Anne intervened. 'He needs to feed his body; my sister can take him onto the terrace.'

Miss Trout shook her head. 'No, she's got a bad foot, the Wing Commander pranged her undercarriage so to speak. I'll put this ice on it.'

'Oh, then I'll help the poor man! I'll feed him!' volunteered Mrs Neugent.

Charles declined the offer. 'I'll put some ice in a cotton serviette and apply it to her foot out on the terrace, she can eat whilst sitting on that chair I put outside earlier.'

Charles took the ice off Miss Trout, and helped the now hobbling Sally onto the terrace.

10: 30 P.M.

In the lounge, the main topic of conversation became the benefits of spreading culture amongst the masses.

The General was at the centre of the debate. 'Well, it's one thing getting them to listen to a brass band or piano or such like, but ballet, no it's just not natural. Ladies in little cute costumes, fair enough, but men in tights, and I mean tight tights, prancing about the stage, well it's not, well natural. If I had any of that sort in the regiment I would...'

The debate continued.

Charles turned to Sally. 'Which foot is it?' They both burst out laughing.

'We should have some food, before we faint, let's see what the good General and Katie have left.'

Twenty minutes later they both had finished their meal. Both were relaxing together smoking, whilst Charles massaged Sally's imaginary injury. *Well,* he thought, *might as well take advantage.* They were both looking at the stars, the moon having moved towards the front of the detached house.

Charles turned to Sally. 'Drink?'

'Why not, I have been stood on after all.'

'I'll get two—'

'Yes, that would be fine, but you'll need a tray.'

Charles entered the lounge and Anne came over, looking concerned. 'Is she alright dear?'

'She's fine, nothing broken.'

'Well, what were you two doing?'

Charles thought for a moment, before saying, 'I, eh, Miss Trout sort of and I—'

'Silly man, look, Joan and Daisy have served coffee, and will soon serve the after-dinner drinks, you concentrate on my sister's well-being.'

He smiled; he was happy to do that task. Anne rejoined the discussion on the artist, Monet.

Frank Beesley was leading the discussion. 'Yes, Mrs Bish and I, I mean Anne and I, thoroughly enjoyed the exhibition, didn't we?' Looking for confirmation from Anne.

'Yes, a fine exhibition, and so well laid out, a must for anyone looking for spiritual enlightenment.'

Frank nodded enthusiastically. 'I couldn't have put it better myself.'

He put his hand on Anne's arm and briefly took her to one side, saying, 'Mrs Bishop—'

'Please, call me Anne, I've told you before.'

'Anne if you would like it, I could draw up a comprehensive list of exhibitions and art galleries for us to visit, I don't know whether you know, but I have contacts, and we can gain access to many select galleries.'

'That would be wonderful Frank, so you do lists, how organized you must be, not like my husband! Telephone me tomorrow afternoon, and we will make arrangements.'

They returned to their group, now discussing Picasso.

The General was scratching his head. 'Well, if that's art, then I'm a china man. I bet he would be no good at painting a nissen hut.'

11:05 P.M.

Five minutes elapsed before Charles returned. Sally didn't mind, this had been the best night for years.
  'Two large black coffees, and two cognacs, as ordered Mistress.'
  'What about the milk?'
  Charles pulled a face, Sally laughed. 'Only joking.'
  They sat in silence drinking their coffee, sipping their VSOP, and gazing at the stars.
  Having finished her drinks, Sally turned to Charles. 'Charlie, you know Anne didn't like, well you know, well, neither did William much.'
  Charles was amazed. 'With someone like you, I find that hard to believe.'
  Sally smiled. 'You're very sweet. Well, you know I always wanted children.'
  'Yes, Sally, just like me.'
  'Well, I often thought that you, Charles, could have—'
  Charles was becoming uneasy about the direction of the conversation given the circumstances, and butted in by asking, 'Do you remember THAT day, 5 years ago?'
  'Of course,' she replied, 'it started so badly, then so well, and finally so badly as I remember it.'
  'Yes, Bill wouldn't go with you to see the gynaecologist so I took you. He was feeling a bit

fragile about the whole problem of you not, well you know.'

'Yes, I certainly do, he did not want me to go. He said there was no problem and when I suggested that he may be the problem, he went, well, nuts. I will not go into details, but this had put a great strain on our relationship, and in particular we parted company that morning on very bad terms.'

'Oh, Sally, I did not know it was so bad, I'm so sorry!' and he held her hand tightly and kissed her cheek.

Charles continued the story. 'So, I agreed to come with you for well, moral support. Then there was the fiasco with the doctor.'

Sally laughed. 'Yes, he thought you were my husband, and after examining me, wanted to see you.'

Yes, I was sitting in the waiting room minding my own business, when he prances out in his white coat and stethoscope, and marches me into a room, puts me in a cubical and tells me to undress. Well, I never say no to a medic, being in the RAF, so complied, ready to give a cough or something. Next thing I know, he's giving me a good examination below the waist, and after a few tut tuts, and squeezes and so on, not going into detail, gives me a clean bill of health.'

Sally took over the story. 'Yes, then he calls me into the room, sits me down next to you, with you naked, and asks me to remove my robe once he's left the room! We just couldn't believe it!'

Charles laughed. 'I shouted, "No, this isn't right! We can't do that, it's not the done thing!" and you closed your eyes whilst I tried to find my underwear!'

Sally giggled. 'The Doctor was startled and asks us, "Now what's the matter with the two of you, Mr and Mrs Brown? You've got all the correct equipment as far as I can tell, there shouldn't be a problem, you are husband and wife, so it's completely natural. I'll do the normal sperm count," pointing to the small bottle, "but quite frankly, I think it's either a psychological or mechanical issue. Just relax and let nature take its course. That's what I do with my wife!" but of course we weren't happy at all!'

Charles nodded. 'Yes, Sally, then you say.'

They both said it together, 'OK Doc, I can confirm that I'm a wife and he's a husband, but I'm not his wife, and he's not my husband!'

They both burst out laughing.

Charles recovered first. 'The Doc slumped into his chair, shouting, "Well, where the hell is your husband, Mrs Brown?" and we looked at each other and laughed.'

Sally chuckled again. 'I replied, "He's at home being comforted by this man's wife! She's good at that sort of thing!" He was stunned.'

Charles nodded. 'The Doctor's face went red, "Oh, comforting eh, that's what you call it do you? Well, there's nothing I can do to help if your marriages are like that. I've heard of this sort of wife swapping arrangement but never come across it in the flesh so to speak. Just get dressed and stop wasting my time. Sort your emotions and marriages out. If you are married to the wrong people do something about it, that's my advice. Now leave!" and so we did!'

Then they became subdued, knowing the advice was excellent but impossible to implement given the events that followed.

Charles sighed. 'Well, eventually everything was cleared up, and with all our clothes on, we returned to this very house, where Anne had been consoling Bill. Oh, Sally, I never told you this, but the Doc took me aside as I was leaving and said, "In a way I admire and resent your way of life young man, I've often thought it might be exciting, but, well, basically, I don't think any one would want to handle my wife in any sort of intimate way! Never the less, if you have one of those wife swapping parties, please let me know, here's my card!" I felt so sorry for him! Mind you, our marriages were not a bed of roses at that time either!'

Sally laughed. 'And during the journey back, following seeing your exposed body, I got this burning desire to, well, you know.'

'Hum, yes indeed I know, I was there too,' said Charles.

Sally sighed. 'But of course, our lives changed forever when we returned to your house. Anne said that five minutes previously, an inconsolable poor William had rushed out of the house and taken his fast car for a spin. We were all very worried. Later that day, there was that knock on the front door and Anne let in a police woman who sat me down and told me that William had crashed his car into a tree, instantly killing himself.'

They both sat in silence for a while.

Sally turned to Charles. 'Was it my fault? I've felt so guilty ever since, and so confused and lost.'

Charles took her in his arms. 'No, it was not, and I'm so sorry.'

He kissed her on the lips just as Anne walked in on them. Anne looked unnaturally amused, Charles and Sally looked ashamed and muddled.

11: 35 P.M.

Anne laughed. 'At last. How long has this been going on?' 5 years?

The two shook their heads as one, looking at their shoes.

'Oh, I see, longer!'

They nodded.

'And you never?'

They shook their heads again. Anne burst out laughing loudly. She could not stop. Suddenly there was a complete release of tension and all three laughed loudly. Half the guests rushed in wondering what had happened. Anne reacted quickly.

'Nothing to worry about, just a family joke,' she shouted towards the open terrace doors, 'Joan, more drinks for my guests please. Please go back inside, I'll be back soon.'

Once they had all left, Anne turned to Charles. 'Charles, fetch another chair.'

Charles did as commanded, and returned with a chair. He was sure he would be packing his bags shortly. *I wonder whether Winston will be thrown out too!*

Anne sat down and turned to her sister, and took her hands in hers. 'I overheard the last bit of your conversation and I have to tell you—'

Sally was very embarrassed and interjected quickly, 'Where from?'

'From when you returned to the house.'

Sally relaxed thinking, *well that's OK then.*

Anne continued. 'You must not feel guilty about William's death. It was not your fault at all, it was mine!'

Sally just could not assimilate this latest bombshell, and slid off her chair with the shock, just as Charles returned with a chair for himself under his arm, shouting, 'Anne, you've not hit her, have you?'

Anne knelt and pulled her sister back onto her chair, and then got off her knees and turned to Charles. 'No, as if I would! She's just had a terrible shock. Get us three brandies dear, and make them doubles.'

Charles, confused as normal in such emotional turmoil, did as asked, and soon returned carrying a tray with three brandy glasses.

'What no ice?' Anne queried.

Charles just shrugged his shoulders. 'Sally and I don't take ice.'

Anne sighed. 'I know, but I do.'

'Oh, do you?'

Anne teased Charles. 'You see, you can't even remember that!'

'Sorry Anne.'

Sally took a sip or three and started coming round.

'Thank you, I'm fine now really,' Sally said.

Anne took her sister's hands again. 'And this shock on top of your poor foot. Which was it now? Your left, I think, oh no, its your right.'

Anne was looking at the compress on Sally's right ankle. Sally looked every inch a guilty sinner.

Anne continued. 'Let me enlighten you both on those events on "that day" as you called it.'

Sally looked bemused, thinking, *just a minute, she said she didn't hear all that about the doctor, but she had.* Sally went red with the thought of her sister knowing those facts.

Anne continued. 'As you both know, William and I were both close spiritually, and spent many a happy day at a museum, art gallery or church. We were very much alike.'

Charles was starting to feel that something had gone on behind his back for years without his knowledge. He felt betrayed. 'How close, dear?'

'Oh, don't worry Charles, not that sort of close, well, not until that day.'

Both Sally and Charles sat up, and stared at each other, then at Anne.

Anne continued. 'Yes, that has been my dirty secret for all these years. I have felt so guilty about it, and many times wished to tell you both. But there's more.'

Sally raised her voice. 'MORE?'

Anne nodded. 'I'm ashamed to say yes. So, this is my full confession. As you both know from your own individual marriage experiences, I believe neither William nor I liked the physical side of, well, let's say certain aspects, of marriage. But that day, William was feeling so vulnerable and I was the only one there to console him. In fact, I think, I was the only one who could from an emotional point of view. Now, let me think how to say it, yes, we were both sat on that large old sofa in the conservatory, you know the one with the quilt I made on it, the one with the red roses and—'

Sally butted in. 'Yes, YES we get the picture.'

Anne sighed. 'Don't interrupt me, I'll lose the thread and the will to tell you everything, now where was I?'

Charles was next to but in. 'Just get on with it, dear, you were on that sofa, then what?'

Anne continued. 'We were on the sofa (Charles nearly screamed, thinking, *if she gets them on that blasted sofa one more time, I'll…*), and he had his head on my, eh, chest, and I was stroking his hair. He was so, so, upset. His manhood was being questioned you see, and he could not bare it. He had always been able to accept that the problem was all Sally's and not his, but now the full truth would come out and he may be found to be the guilty party. He could never understand why it was so important you see. Why make such a fuss about nothing? Why try and make out that he was not a real man? He was talking like this, and then he said "I think Sally has always preferred Charles, I should have married you, Anne!" And he started crying.'

Now everyone was feeling remorseful.

Anne continued. 'Suddenly, William turned to me, and confessed "Actually", he said "I have always preferred you to Sally" and he kissed me on the lips. Well, one thing led to another and afterwards we felt so bad about what we had done. Yes, I suppose we agreed it had been quite nice, but we were now racked with guilt.'

Charles stood up; he had heard enough. 'I'm off for a smoke.'

Anne got to her feet, and grabbed him by the jacket sleeve. 'No, you're not, I'm so sorry, but there's more. I must finish. Sit down, please.'

12: 05 A.M.

Charles grudgingly put his cigarette back in its pack.
    Anne paced up and down, then seemingly having decided what to say next, continued. 'I made us both strong coffees and we sat politely next to each other in some sort of mental discomfort. Suddenly William jumped up. "I've spoilt everything. I've spoilt our friendship and my marriage and been a traitor to my best friend. I've got to get out of here and think things through." I said that I had something to do with it as well, but he was inconsolable. "I'm off for a drive," he shouted, "I need to clear my head. I'm so sorry Anne, sorry for everything, and please tell Sally that." And he picked up his keys and stormed out of the house. A few minutes later I could hear his car wheels spinning on our gravel drive, and looking out the window, saw the car speeding round the corner at the end of the road. That was the last time I saw him alive. The rest you know. So, you see it's all my fault, I am the guilty party here, I have carried this responsibility for years, and I'm sorry to both of you that I have not confessed before.'
    Anne started to cry.
    Charles went to her, and although the revelations had been to say the least, devastating, was able to give her a hug. He then paced up and down, scratching his head. *I must think things through logically. I'm now in possession of all the facts, and just like I did when*

carrying out my, well let's say, pastoral duties as a wing commander, should be able to reach a conclusion that all parties can live with. At the end of the day, I always believe that since you can't change the past, you must just learn to live with it, and look forward to a brighter future. He was very good at this sort of post-mission review. Many a time he had a grown man on the other side of his desk breaking down in front of him because of this or that, whether it was not defending his leader when being the wingman, or seeing the actual reality of war in the shape of blood and body parts rather than just damaged machines, or just getting lost on patrol and getting back to base to find most of your pals were never going to return. *Yes, guilt was a mental killer and it eats your soul if you let it. It had been my job to mend the broken souls of pilots and get then back in their planes, and I'll try and do the same for Anne and Sally!* He chuckled softly, thinking, *but I won't expect them to fly a Spitfire!*

Charles announced, 'I'm off for a smoke, and a think, back in five minutes with the solution to our woes!'

Charles left, leaving the two women with their thoughts.

Charles went through the kitchen where Joan was humming whilst washing up. 'Oh, it's you Mr Charles. I just have to say that poor Anne's sister is acting mighty strange to say the least.'

Charles breezed past replying, 'Remember, Joan, it's THAT anniversary!'

Joan dropped a plate, which smashed on the draining board. 'Oh, I'm so sorry, I didn't remember. Poor lamb, she must be all at sixes and sevens.'

'And eights, nines and tens,' Charles shouted from the utility room, on his way to the back door and garden.

Outside, he stood for a while, looking at the stars, all was quiet except for a slight rustling from the direction of the dahlias. He got his cigarette case out, took a cigarette, tapped it on the case, and searched for his lighter in his jacket left pocket. There was another slight rustle but this time, nearby, this time from the azaleas. Charles wondering what it was, and being distracted, dropped his lighter. He stooped down, feeling with his hands in the dark, hoping to locate it. There was a louder rustle and then an ear-piercing 'MEOW' from behind him. Charles only had time to think, *stupid man, you've left your tail exposed, you idiot.* Then a large hairy concrete block with raised claws sprang through the air and landed on his back.

'MEOW. HISS. MEOW.'

Charles stood upright with the cat still digging in. 'Agh, get off you hairy beast.'

The monstrous tortoiseshell cat held on; he was enjoying himself.

'Winston, I mean it, get off NOW or its no nibbles for a week.'

Winston understood from the tone of his voice that it was time to disengage his claws. He let go, landed on all four paws, wandered over to the step, tail erect, sat down and cleaned his claws, whilst purring loudly.

Winston was thinking cat thoughts, which loosely translated were, *I love my non-cat servant. He feeds me, strokes me, lets me sit on his lap, and plays with me, but most importantly, he feeds me! I'm so lucky! Oh, I wonder whether it's time for my second supper yet? I've lots to do tonight and so little time! That ginger tom-cat needs taking down a peg or two, he's getting very bold!*

Charles sat down next to him. 'You swine, Winnie, but you certainly got me that time. I always watched my six when flying, but my guard was down then, that's for sure!'

He gave Winnie a tickle under his chin. Winston was just a small stray kitten when Charles first met him. Now he was probably the largest tom-cat in London and king of the neighbourhood. Charles laughed to himself. Nicely behaved dogs adopted other flyers, but it was just his luck to be lumbered with a psycho feline. Winnie was knocking on a bit now, but he still had plenty of attitude. Charles laughed again, and got up.

Charles' back was stinging from the claw wounds. 'Come on old boy, nibbles time.'

Winnie raced to the back door tail erect. In the kitchen, Joan had just finished washing up and was getting the coffee cups ready.

'Oh, not that furry dustbin. Oh well, Mr Bishop, there's some left overs in the fridge.'

Charles gave Winnie some chicken, and then removed his jacket.

'Why, Mr Bishop there's blood on the back of your shirt.'

Charles winced. 'I'm afraid I've been the victim of a big cat attack.'

Joan came over to him all concerned. 'Oh, poor man, take the shirt off and let me take a look.'

He obeyed.

Joan looked sternly at Winnie. 'Naughty kitty. I'll get some ointment and sort you out sir, just bend over the table.'

She soon returned with some sort of soothing ointment, and started to apply it on the wounds.

It was then that Daisy entered the kitchen. 'Why, Joan, what's going on 'ere then? Surely this isn't part of your domestic duties!'

Joan turned to her. 'Silly girl, nothing like that. He's been attacked by a wild animal called Winston.'

Daisy came over and looked at the wounds. 'Poor man, but a lovely physique,' and commenced stroking Charles's hair in an attempt to sooth his pain.

Sally and Anne, having got impatient, burst in just as Charles was saying, 'Ah, that feels so good. You certainly have a gentle touch, Joan.'

Sally was the first to speak, Anne was speechless as she absorbed the scene of her husband half naked whilst two women were massaging his back and stroking his hair.

'What's going on here then?' Sally enquired.

Joan jumped back and dropped the ointment. Daisy let go of his hair. Winnie went over to inspect the tube of ointment, but was very disappointed with its smell, *nothing to eat here,* he thought, so went and sat in his basket and watched the non-cats whilst he washed himself.

Charles pointed to the cat and turned around so the ladies could see his clawed back. 'That crazy cat attacked me in the garden.'

Anne laughed and exclaimed, 'Well, stop playing with Winnie and Joan and Daisy, get another shirt from the laundry room, and join us on the terrace. We need to reach a conclusion about a certain situation.'

Anne took Sally by the arm and returned to the terrace where she explained about their problem cat. 'He has another trick where he would climb up poor Charles' leg if he thinks he's being ignored. But then again, he has a softer side. One day I found him in his dog kennel curled up with 4 stray kittens. He hates other cats, hunts anything including dogs and foxes, but adores kittens. If you want Charles, you'll have to put up with Winston. I suggest a lot of bribery involving sardines and chicken. Do you have any thick long socks? Oh, by the way, has Charles told you about Winston being a war hero? If not, ask him.'

12: 40 A.M.

Charles returned to the terrace fully clothed. 'I've reached an obvious conclusion; we are all to blame for our actions. All four of us made some wrong decisions, some wrong choices, and had some incompatible feelings. None of us fully knew the consequences. If we can agree to a new regime, and be united for once in our grief, and our love and respect for each other, then William's death will not be in vain. From today onwards, we must look forward to a better future. No more thinking and worrying about the past. But, since we are all being truthful, I have, I'm very sorry to say, one further revelation.'

He told the girls about that fateful night in the pub. 'You must see that it was me and Bill who owe you an apology. So, perhaps you could say it was my fault for suggesting the draw, or Bill's for picking the paper, or you Anne for not liking the whole baby thing, or you Sally for wanting a family, or Bill for agreeing to marry you Sally, need I go on? My conclusion is that we look forward now, and never back. That's what Bill would have wanted.'

The two sisters considered his words, then got to their feet, and hugged each other, with Sally saying, 'Sorry sister! Let's forgive and forget!'

Anne nodded saying, 'Yes, let's all be friends and live our lives the way we want to from now on! No compromises!'

Sally then went over to Charles and slapped his face. 'That's for that stupid draw,' and then gave him a hug.

Anne announced, 'Tomorrow morning we will have a lot to discuss about the future domestic arrangements and so forth, including the fact that you may be seeing a lot more of Frank Beesley. In the meantime, Sally, why not stay the night, in fact why not move in with us. I really don't mind!'

She gave a sly look towards Charles. 'Now I must get back to my guests. It's time for final coffees. Then we can hopefully get rid of our guests!'

12; 50 A.M.

Charles and Sally both sat down on the chairs.
'Another drink, Sally dearest?'
'Yes darling, but, Charlie, first can I ask a delicate question?'
'I suppose, I think tonight's the night for full disclosure.'
'Charles, did you ever get a report on your sperm—'
She stopped speaking immediately as Miss Trout and her girl friend known only as Gerry, skipped in hand in hand giggling, catching Charles massaging Sally's right toes.
Miss Trout blushed, and let go of her companion's hand. 'Ops, we thought the terrace was free!'
Charles dropped Sally's right leg and her heel hit a terrace paving slab. Sally yelped.
'Oh, sorry are we interrupting anything?' Miss Trout studied the scene, as Charles now rubbed Sally's right heel. 'Just a moment, wasn't it your left foot that needed attention? Yes, I'm right. Gerry, you be Mrs Brown at the piano and I'll be me, now—'
Charles stopped her before the investigations got to the truth. 'Ladies, its such a lovely night, and we need coffee, so we will leave you alone with the stars.'
He helped Sally up and took the hobbling patient into the lounge. He turned and saw the two girls

holding hands again, then they embraced and kissed. *Lucky them,* he thought.

The guests were being served more after-dinner drinks and coffee. The conversation had turned to the new art exhibition at the Tate exploring spiritual rebirth, confession, forgiveness, and redemption.

The General was out of his depth. 'Cods wallop, that's what I say. Nothing like real life, now, if anyone in my regiment wanted forgiveness, soul-searching, or such like, I would give them extra guard duty and a ten-mile march. Nothing like a bit of discipline and pain for curing any deep thinking. One thing the army detests is deep thinkers. Those sorts tend to disobey orders! I used to tell my men an order is an order and however ridiculous it may be, it must be obeyed without question!'

Anne shook her head. 'Dear, Ernest, you're so wrong. Why, just tonight in this house all four were played out. Sometimes it's essential for our well-being, just ask Father O'Neil!'

The General shrugged his shoulders. 'Well, perhaps I'm just an old codger with the soul of a banana.'

All those present agreed, but said nothing.

Frank was next to speak, 'Well, it will be a fine exhibition, and Anne and I think…'

The discussion continued.

Charles was beginning to wonder whether this party was going to turn into an all-nighter.

Anne came over looking concerned, Charles pointed to Sally's right foot. 'It's playing up again.'

'Are you sure?' Anne was a bit sceptical.

'Yes, I dropped her foot on the terrace floor.'

'If you say so. Take her into the kitchen and get some ice on it.'

1: 15 A.M.

Charles sat Sally down on one of the kitchen chairs and put an ice compress on her ankle. 'Is that any better?'

He sat down beside her and she put her head on his chest. 'Much.'

Charles quickly looked in the direction of Winston, but luckily, he was fast asleep.

Sally saw the concern in his face. 'What's wrong dearest?'

Charles just had to tell Sally the truth. 'It's Winnie you see, he gets very jealous and protective especially if he doesn't know the person well. You will have to be very careful in his presence.'

Sally was starting to think that Charles might have to choose between her and that blasted cat. 'What can I do to gain his trust and love?'

'Easy, food. You will have to take over feeding duties. One bit of advice though, don't get your fingers too close to his teeth, just drop the bowl and stand well back. In fact, you may find oven gloves jolly useful to start with. Joan will help. She's an expert, and has the wounds to prove it!'

Sally was still curious about what Anne had said. 'Charles, what did Anne mean when she said that Winston was a war hero?'

Charles had a think for a few minutes. 'Well, its all governed by the Official Secrets Act and so forth, so all I can say is that Winnie had a tendency to follow me everywhere when a kitten, and on a few occasions ended up as a stow-away on my aircraft. Bill even ended up making him a flying suit and helmet.'

'Yes, my husband was always good with a needle and thread.'

Charles resumed his tale. 'On one night-mission, Winnie managed to help shoot down a German bomber by playing about near the gun trigger, and on another, he managed to kill a German SS officer after he and I were shot down behind enemy lines. He just happened to be cleaning his bits and pieces one night on a footpath in Belgium when an unobservant Nazi fell over him in the dark, and cracked his head on the cobbles. Winnie's got medals to prove it, presented by Winston Churchill himself!'

Sally couldn't believe it. 'You're joking of course.'

Charles shook his head. 'No, I swear on Bill's grave, the medals are in one of my desk drawers, but I won't show you, since Winnie is so modest, and you will just accuse him of boasting and being an insensitive beast.'

Sally hit Charles playfully on the ear.

After a few minutes of reflection, Sally sighed. 'Charlie, as I was asking, did you ever get a report on your sperm—'

Suddenly Joan burst in. 'More coffee, more coffee,' she grumbled, 'oh I didn't see you there Mr Bishop, oh, and you too, Mrs Bishop.'

Sally turned round.

'Oh no, its you, Mrs Brown, so sorry, I thought with you both so, well, in any case it can't be her, otherwise she would be in two places at once since she sent me to get more coffee, but dear me, you both look so much alike, except for your dress sense of course. Very daring choice, Mrs Brown, if I may be so bold, but then you can get away with it I suppose. But then I say, just because you've got it, don't mean you must flaunt it.'

Charles stopped any reply from Sally by gripping her arm, as she was rising to the bait. 'May we have two coffees whilst you're at it, Joan?'

'Of course, anything for you Wing Commander.'

Sally whispered something about another smitten admirer in Charles's ear, at the same time giving it a nibble. Charles gave out a little yelp of surprise.

'Oh, Sir, what's the problem, is it your poor back? Is it hurting? I'm quire happy to put some more ointment on, just remove—'

'No, that won't be necessary, I'm fine, Sal, eh, Mrs Brown just stood on my foot.'

Joan saw an opportunity to help her hero. 'I'll get some ice.'

Charles smiled. 'Thank you, you're very kind.'

Joan turned her back and went to the freezer. Sally nibbled Charles's ear again. He yelped.

'Oh dear,' Joan's back seemed to say, 'that must be really painful. You really must be more careful, Mrs Brown, him being a hero and such like. Now sir, which foot is it?'

'Oh, er, my left.'

Joan scratched her head and shook it. 'Well, that's odd, since as Mrs Brown is sat on your right, how come it's your left foot? Surly, it should be your right foot! What were you doing to him Mrs Brown? He's a war hero, and he's a married man! Just leave him alone!' and she tutted as she applied the ice pack.

Joan then went back to making the coffee.

Sally giggled as she went for Charles's ear again.

Joan turned round and looked sternly at Sally. 'It's nothing to laugh about, Mr Bishop is supposed to be playing golf tomorrow. He won't be able to whack his balls proper-good the way you're treating him.'

Both Charles and Sally looked at each other and giggled.

Joan tut-tutted, and left with the coffee jug grumbling about some people being too drunk for their own good. Charles and Sally both sat silently for a while, drinking the coffee, both with ice packs on their offending foot.

'Charlie, as I was saying—'

The General walked in. 'Oh, it's you two again, I don't suppose you could direct me—'

Charles raised his right arm. 'Next on the left and please close the door behind you.'

The General left and closed the door.

'Now what were you asking?'

'I was only asking if the doctor ever sent you—'

The door opened revealing a troubled man. Sally screamed in frustration.

Frank Beesley looked at them both. 'Oh, wrong door, sorry, urgent need, too much coffee. Sorry to disturb, foot still hurting, eh? I've got some ointment that will help with that, I'll give it to Anne tomorrow.'

Charles looked at him severely. 'Next on the left, but the General's on the throne at the moment. You can always go upstairs, second on the right!'

Frank looked very flustered. 'Oh dear, it's just, well, you may not know this but I—'

Both Charles and Sally said together, 'WE know shut the door behind you.'

Charles felt like locking the door.

'Where were we, oh yes, and the answer I think is no, no report.'

Sally thought for a while, before saying, 'Well then, we'll give it a few months, but you must know that my biological clock is ticking like a time bomb and there's not much, well, time left.'

Charles looked at her ankle. 'How's the foot?'

'Oh, much better thanks, the swelling has gone down a lot, and yes, just a bit of bruising.'

'Sorry, Sally dearest!'

'I forgive you, Charlie!'

They both sat in silence, her head on his chest whilst he massaged her ankle.

The door opened and Gerry walked in. Both Charles and Sally said in unison, 'Next on the left, but there's a queue.'

Gerry was confused. 'What's next on the left?'

Charles replied, 'We assume it's the toilet you need.'

Gerry shook her head.

'Oh no, I just want a glass of water.' She went to the sink and poured some tap water in a glass, then turned round.

'Oh, what a lovely pussycat, can I stroke it?'

Winston was now asleep, dreaming of being in a big flying bird with his non-cat servant, and falling from the sky onto a world full of strange smells and large fat pigeons.

'You could stroke him, but I would not recommend it, especially as he's asleep.'

Gerry laughed loudly, waking Winston.

Charles sprang away from Sally, and her head nearly hit the kitchen table.

'Oh, cats love me, it's always been that way,' and Gerry started moving towards the now alert cat.

Charles sprang between the two. 'How are your reflexes young lady?'

'Oh, fine.'

Charles looked her in the eyes. 'Then just move slowly towards him, but be ready to retreat quickly, and don't turn your back on him whatever you do. But remember, you have been warned, so don't blame me if he attacks!'

'Oh, tosh,' Gerry replied, and she continued towards the cat, which was now vocalizing something between a growl and a meow, ears set back, fur raised.

Gerry smiled, and started gently clicking her left fingers and making a sound like a distressed sparrow. She turned her head towards Charles, saying, 'You've just got to reassure the animal! It's just scared!' Then she turned back, bent down and looked at the hissing Winston. 'There, kitty, it's alright, Aunty Gerry loves you.'

Charles felt he must issue a final warning, 'Miss, that cat is never scared, stop sounding like his prey, and definitely don't hold out your hand, it's bite size!'

Gerry wasn't in the mood for advice. She extended her left arm and hand, and Winston fixed his eyes on the end of the longest finger. Gerry went to touch his back, and Winston's right paw flashed from right to left like a high-speed scythe. Gerry's reflexes were excellent, and Winston only managed to get one claw on target.

'Ouch,' Gerry screamed, dropping the glass in her right hand.

Charles jumped forward and caught it before it could smash and release its contents. One thing Winnie hated was getting wet.

'Well done, Gerry, now move backwards towards the door, NO don't turn round. You must face him. Ask Joan for the first aid box!'

Gerry did as she was told, felt for the doorknob, and left.

Charles shouted through the door, 'I suggest a large brandy as well, some for the wound and some for your nerves.'

Peace resumed. Winston was purring as he had a quick wash and scratch, and then settled down again, thinking, *I'm enjoying tonight!*

Sally's nerves were also on edge. 'Any chance of a drink?'

Charles nodded. 'Good idea, two brandies and coffees coming up.

2: 00 A.M.

It took the brandy and five minutes for Sally to calm down. She started thinking about recent discussions. Sally was looking down the dark passage that led first to the pantry, and then to the conservatory. It was all in darkness, other than the starlight shining through its glass roof, giving the room an eerie pale blue sheen.

'Charlie, talking about not wasting time, you know that sofa in the conservatory with the quilt made by Anne on it, the one with roses and—'

Charles leapt to his feet and took her hand, 'Good idea. Let's give it a go!'

They both went into the conservatory, and Sally shut the door to the kitchen. 'I don't want us to be disturbed by Winston.'

Charles shook his head. He went back to the door, and turned the key. 'Sorry, my love, but Winston has learnt how to open doors. One high leap and two stout paws is all he needs. Luckily however, he has not yet learnt how to pick locks.'

2: 40 A.M.

Some 30 minutes later, Sally and Charles were back in the kitchen relaxing, drinking coffee and contemplating.

Mrs Neugent burst in. 'Oh, there you are, you naughty man, where have you been and what have you been up to?'

Charles blushed, he thought for a few seconds that she had observed something. 'Hello, Mrs Neugent, um, I mean, Katie, yes here I am.'

'You promised to play again.'

Charles stood up smiling. 'Katie, I'll play anything with you, you know that, what would you like to do?'

Katie Neugent giggled. 'Oh, you silly boy! You know what I meant, play the piano again!'

Sally giggled.

'Oh, Mrs Brown, I see you are feeling better, although a bit flushed, perhaps you are coming down with something.'

Charles linked his arm in Katie Neugent's. 'Let's go and see what we can play.'

As they walked, Katie Neugent giggled again. 'I want you to come to my Hall, next weekend and play some more. Even the mayor is coming, along with a certain naval VIP.'

'Katie, I'll play in whichever room you want, but will there be enough room in your hall for a piano as well as your guests? Perhaps your lounge would be better.'

'Oh, you awful boy! I'm having a weekend house party at Bleak Hall, it's on the south downs just south of Crawley. And of course, bring Anne with you, and,' pointing at Sally, 'I suppose Mrs Brown if you wish, although I suggest she dresses more conservatively and minds her Ps and Qs for a change!'

'Oh, I wish alright, Mrs Brown turns my music sheets you know and makes sure I'm on beat. I couldn't do it without her. I'll get her to wear a long dress!'

Katie Neugent shook her head, saying, 'It's the top bit that I'm worried about! She does tend to show up at parties over exposed in the, well, to say bluntly, the chest department. My VIP will not be able to take his eyes off her, being a Royal Navy type, and we don't want any nonsense or incidents getting back to The Palace, do we?'

Sally giggled again, as she followed them into the sitting room.

Charles laughed. 'Of course not, I'm sure Mrs Brown will be on her best behaviour! I'll keep a tight grip on her, and make sure she's not over-exposed in public!'

Katie Neugent thought for a few seconds, then turned towards Sally. 'Oh, fine, then you can come too, Mrs Brown. I don't suppose you can sing at all?'

Sally followed them into the lounge replying, 'Well, I did sing in my school's production of The Mikado. I played a Japanese girl called Yum-Yum, and sang silly songs about three little maids, a blazing sun, and such like!'

Charles was impressed. 'I never knew that. Which character did Anne play?'

'Why, the Lord High Executioner as well as the assistant stage director.'

Charles laughed. 'Of course, she would, wouldn't she! I'm sure she was magnificent.'

Sally had to laugh. 'She sang flat, but her voice could be heard throughout the County of Sussex.'

They were now next to the piano. Charles thought, *I should ask Mrs Neugent where her damn Hall is!* 'Katie, where exactly is this Hall of yours?'

'Oh, Charles, of course, you've not been before! Anne comes regularly for a game of bridge and afternoon tea, but you've only ever flown over it!'

2: 50 A.M.

Charles was thinking as he sat down on the piano stool. 'Just a minute Katie, you don't mean that huge pile of bricks on top of the hill close to the Biggin Hill airfield?'

Katie Neugent smiled. 'Yes, that's it, the terrible decrepit monstrosity that my late, and even more decrepit, husband, Rufus, inherited.'

Charles continued, although he knew he would regret it later. 'We used to use it during the war as a way-point when flying back to Biggin. I remember there was usually an old crusty chap on the large front lawn waving his walking stick enthusiastically at me as I flew low overhead, carrying his shotgun under his other arm, with two black dogs by his side. He was certainly happy to see me fly over.'

Katie Neugent shook her head. 'If you could have heard the obscenities coming from his mouth, you would have thought differently. He hated the noise. In the end he resorted to taking pot-shots at the planes but luckily, he never downed one.'

The General had been over-hearing the conversation and joined in. 'Ah, the Major, terrible shot, but excellent in a crisis although he often caused it. Still, he had a fine wine cellar, and didn't put up with any nonsense from the lower ranks. Why, I remember that whenever he had any of his German prisoners bleating about the Geneva Convention, he would take their ba—'

Katie interrupted quickly, 'In the end he was killed in a shooting accident.'

Charles reluctantly responded, 'Oh, shot himself then?'

'Oh no, he was shot by Blackie his gun dog.'

Sally could not resist. 'You should never give a dog a gun you know, it's so dangerous. Did Blackie have a gun license?'

Katie ignored Sally. Long ago, she had found this the best policy when it came to this annoying woman. 'Rufus was on the lawn as usual when a flight of Spitfires flew over. Rufus let loose with his 12-bore shot gun, but as usual missed, and was just reloading when I joined him with his mid-morning whisky and soda. He was shouting at the planes, and then he turned to me and said, "What the hell have you been doing with my gun? The barrels must be bent or something." I upset him by talking back, suggesting it may be his eyesight. He just lost his rag, and threw his gun at me. It flew over my head and both Blackie and Midnight, being gun dogs, chased after it. Blackie grabbed the gun first just as it hit the ground, and returned it to her master. Rufus took hold of the barrels in both hands and pulled hard, but Blackie's teeth must have got stuck on the trigger, and the gun went off.'

Charles had to seem concerned, 'Oh, you must have been so upset, and surely miss him dearly.'

Katie nodded. 'Yes, I miss the old boring goat that's for sure as I'm really enjoying life now, and since I married Luigi, my life has changed completely. He's so cultured and Italian. Of course, I was very upset at the time, you see my husband's blood ruined my favourite white dress, and poor Blackie was inconsolable, she just sat next to his body howling away. It was so sad; it took days for her to start eating again. Still, we gave him a good send off. Luigi had organized everything and it was such a wonderful day. It was probably the best day of my life at the time! My husband, was Eustace Rufus by name, and useless by nature, and was as lively as a slug, unless of course, when you lot came flying over, or when we ran out of single malt!'

The General interjected, 'Yes, Luigi may be a bit well, a bit of a light weight and foreign, but he certainly knows how to throw a good party and his knowledge of wine is second to none.'

Charles knew he shouldn't ask, but was in a devilish mood, 'Who the blazes is this Luigi character?'

Katie Neugent's face turned the colour of beetroot. 'He was a prisoner of war and became our gardener. It seems that with him coming from an important family in Sicily, certain strings were pulled and he was let out of prison into the care of my Rufus. Rufus hated Luigi at first, him being Italian and all, but certain threats had been made from up on high, and what with Luigi being so knowledgeable about fine wine and how to procure it in times of war along with certain other luxuries like cigars and single malts, a sort of truce and understanding between the two of them became established.'

Katie Neugent whispered, 'I will not say much more than this, Rufus spent much of his time drinking, smoking, and taking pot-shots at aircraft, and I spent a great deal of time with Luigi in the garden, and during the evenings, in the Orangery sitting on the old sofa covered in a floral quilt, in front of the fire, and well, what with a glass or two of wine, well, one thing led to—'

'Led to another?' interjected Sally.

Katie Neugent nodded. 'Well, yes, one thing did indeed lead to many others,' and she blushed again and paused for a while whilst she remembered a few of those others on that sofa, before smiling broadly, then clearing her throat and continuing, 'now, and this means you too, Mrs Brown, as our you-know-who naval VIP will be there too, please, well, be discreet.'

Charles was confused. 'You-know-who, who?'

Katie Neugent was astounded. She whispered the name in his ear, then stood up. Charles nodded. Katie Neugent continued. 'He loves playing with my collection of horse carriages. Now, this is important, certain topics of conversation are to be avoided and I'll supply you with a list of these later. Oh, and as regards you, Mrs Brown, I suggest perhaps Anne can help you dress appropriately, you couldn't curtsy in that dress and maintain your dignity.'

Charles grabbed Sally before she could respond, and sat at the piano with Sally by his side. 'Now then, Katie, do you have a ballroom?'

'Oh yes.'

'Then I'll play some waltzes.'

He started with the Minute Waltz, followed by some Strauss Waltzes.

Katie Neugent clapped enthusiastically. 'Yes, we will have a Ball.'

Charles looked at Sally. 'Yes, we certainly will, especially in your orangery!'

Sally giggled.

It was now very late so Charles finished with the first world war song "Good Bye," being a definite favourite of the General's, who started a sing along, followed by a newer one that Charles was learning, playing this time with some music sheets which Sally pretended to be in charge of, "Good night campers". He made Sally sing the words, only to find she had a very sweet voice.

Katie Neugent was ecstatic. 'Oh, what a wonderful voice. Yes, you must come too for sure, I'll send over some of my favourite pieces for piano and soloist. It will be a wonderful cultured evening.'

Charles looked at Sally. 'Well, Katie, we will have a lot to do over the next few days, but with diligent rehearsing, we should become competent. However, I must ask for one favour.'

'Yes, anything dear boy,' Katie Neugent replied.

'You must show us your orangery.'

Sally giggled again.

3: 45 A.M.

All the guests had left leaving Anne, Sally and Charles relaxing on the lounge sofa.

'It's a bit of a squeeze this.' Anne complained, let's go to the conservatory and sit—'

Charles interrupted. 'Oh, um, no its very, eh cold in there.'

Anne looked at Sally, who smiled. 'Oh, Oh, I see.'

They continued to drink their coffee whilst thinking of the evening's events.

Anne spoke first, looking at Sally, 'I suppose you're staying here with what's left of the night? Probably best, it is, well, so late. I'll get you some nightwear, I've a silk number that I've not worn since my, lets think, yes, wedding night. Yes, that will do. It will fit you! Sally, you can sleep in the small back bedroom, and you, Charles can sleep next door to her in that double bedroom at the back of the house overlooking the conservatory. Oh, and Charles, there will be no golf tomorrow, and remember up at ten, there's lots to discuss, so sleep well, and have a good night!' and off she trotted towards the stairs, leaving Charles and Sally with their own thoughts.

Suddenly there was a knock on the front door. Anne rushed down the stairs. 'I'll answer it, it's probably Frank.'

Anne unlocked and opened the door. 'Oh!'

Standing on the doorstep was a tall slender good-looking woman with sort jet-black hair of about 30.

'Sorry to disturb you at this late hour. I've been walking up and down your street for hours trying to get enough courage to knock. Once I saw that all your guests had left, I took the plunge.'

Anne was confused. 'So, how can I help you?'

The stranger looked at Anne closely. 'Well, Mrs Brown, I need to speak to you about William.'

Anne was even more confused. 'I'm Anne her sister, but I suppose you had better come in out of the cold, she's in the living room with my husband.'

Anne led the woman into the lounge.

'This woman wants to speak to you, Sally.'

Both Charles and Sally looked at the stranger.

Charles was first to speak, 'I know you, don't I?'

The woman nodded. 'You certainly do, Wing Commander, I was the squadron leader's wife.'

Charles went over to her, and shook her hand. 'Of course, it's Camilla, isn't it? I seem to remember that you and Bill used to play a lot of golf together in the old days.'

Camilla nodded. 'Yes, and it's been 5 years today since poor Wills' death. I've felt so guilty for all these years, and decided that the time had come to tell, you Sally, what happened that terrible day and why I was responsible for him crashing his car.'

All three were now as alert as a pride of hungry lions.

'If you allow me to sit, I will tell you the sorry tale of how I caused his death.'

Anne announced, 'I'd better get some drinks first!'

73

Within five minutes all four had coffees and large brandies and Camilla was ready to give her confession.

'You see, poor Wills came over to my flat that afternoon for some solace and support, but found only infidelity and betrayal.'

Charles quickly came to the conclusion that this was not going to be a short confession, so got to his feet. 'I'll make some more coffee, but carry on.'

Charles went into the kitchen and sorted out the coffee maker. He thought back to those early days in the squadron. Suddenly he remembered that first dance organized by no less than Camilla. *She certainly had a commanding personality, but too straight a chassis for my taste. I always got the impression that she wore the trousers in the squadron leader's house.* He thought further as the coffee percolated. *Yes, that night I and Bill were together as usual at the dance. I danced with a few women, but Bill just sat and watched. Sometimes I got the distinct impression he would prefer to dance with me! After a few beers, Billy Boy leant over to me and said, "You know, Charlie Boy, I fancy you more than most of the women here. In fact, in strictest confidence, there's just one here that I would be interested in but she's well above my rank!" Yes, then he finished his drink and went to ask Camilla for a dance. I seem to remember them later huddled in a corner in deep conversation. I didn't consider this event too deeply at the time, but now? Perhaps it all makes sense! All that subsequent golf with Camilla, and Bill's continuing close friendship with me. Yes, perhaps he married Sally because I was marrying*

Anne. That way he could guarantee spending a great deal of time with me! And, yes, Charles thought, *if you put a dress on Michael Angelo's David, and a short black-haired wig, then hay presto, Camilla, handsome and beautiful all at the same time.*

Charles rejoined the women with more coffee on a tray.

Camilla was still talking, 'Yes as I said, it started with golf, but one day Wills turned up and the heavens opened, so we sat and talked and had a brandy or three, and one thing—'

Sally interrupted saying, 'led to another?'

Camilla nodded. 'We were very discreet, then Charles and Wills met you two women, and as I would never leave my husband, Wills decided it was time to settle down in a normal relationship. I remember him saying on that final wonderful sunny day, "Cammy, I'll always remember and miss you, but as long as I have Charles, I'll survive!" And after that day we lost touch for quite a while.'

Charles began to feel uncomfortable again. Suddenly a memory sprang up in his confused brain. It had been a lovely sunny day in May 1941 at Biggin on the Bump (as all the RAF chaps called it). Charles and Bill had been sitting in their deck chairs, looking at London.

'Another terrible raid last night,' Charles exclaimed, looking at the rising smoke.

Bill seemed in his own little world, but eventually appeared to make up his mind what to say, 'Charlie, I need to say something, so here goes. The last year with you, has been the best time of my life. I know that sounds strange given the circumstances, but that's it in a nut shell Charlie boy.'

Charles remembered that at the time, he didn't quite know how to reply, 'Well, Billy boy, if it was not for you as my wingman, I would not be here today that's for sure.'

Again, there had been a period of quiet, and then Bill put his arm around Charles's shoulder and said, 'Promise that we will remain close friends after this terrible war!'

Charles remembering that he didn't know what to say next, other than feeling that Bill was behaving very emotionally.

Charles replied, 'Of course, we will always be best friends.'

Both were silent for a while, and Charles remembered looking at Bill, and there was a slight frown on his face.

Charles decided to change the subject. 'Look Bill, I've been thinking, we need to do something about this night bombing. We are spending too much time dwelling on things, now that the situation is quieter. Ever thought about night flying? 68 squadron are looking for recruits to fly Beaufighters, fancy being my co-pilot? How's your night vision, Billy boy?'

Bill slapped Charles on the back, and ruffled his hair, beaming from ear to ear. 'That's suits me fine, Charlie, together we will give the Hun a bloody nose, and scare the living daylights out of them! We'll take

Winnie with us as our mascot! Is he any good with a machine gun?'

Charles came out of his daydream thinking, *yes, the signs were there and can't be denied. If only I had been more attentive at the time.*

'Charles, CHARLES, come back to us and replenish Camilla's drink,' commanded Anne.

Camilla sipped her refilled drink and drank some of the hot dark coffee and continued. 'We never saw each other until the end of May 1945. My husband died of his wounds just after VE day.'

Charles nodded. 'Yes, I was shocked to hear about his death. He was very unfortunate, surviving the war, only to be run over outside Buckingham Palace by the Royal's car containing the Princesses after their night out! Bill and I attended the funeral. Bill remarked how dignified but somehow vulnerable you looked.'

Camilla replied, 'Yes, that's when it started again. We just couldn't resist; we were made for each other. Our tastes regarding certain, well, let's say, intimate matters, were so similar!'

Sally suddenly jumped up and pointed at Camilla. 'Just a moment, I know you, you were Bill's PA at Nuts and Bolts.'

Camilla smiled. 'I certainly was.'

Sally laughed ironically. 'I only met you at the annual office parties, but remember thinking at the time that you, standing next to Bill in your dinner suite, looked more like a male colleague than a secretary.'

'PA, Mrs Brown.' Camilla corrected.

Sally was annoyed at the long-legged so-called woman. 'Secretary, PA, or whatever, it's well, it's all too much.'

Charles put his arm around her and comforted Sally.

Camilla looked on, and pointed her accusing finger at the two of them. 'And what about you two lovebirds? Wills always had his suspicions about you two!'

Anne intervened. 'So that explains all those late nights at the office. Please carry on. Let's get it all out in the open then we can finally move on.'

Camilla continued. 'Well, on that terrible day, Wills, having a key to my flat, burst in, only to find me, well, entertaining. I'm afraid I have quite an appetite you see. Wills was so upset already, but finding me in bed with our friend and colleague, Jules, well what could I say? He shouted, "This is the final straw. I just can't go on living. I made a terrible mistake today with Anne, betraying my one best friend, Charles, and now this!" and he walked out of my flat and out of my life forever.'

Camilla burst into tears. The other three just stared at each other.

Once Camilla had finished her drinks, she got up to go. Charles came over to her, and walked her to the front door.

'I suppose I should thank you for coming and being so illuminating. It seems to me that we must all share some of the blame, and that includes Bill, or Wills as you call him. Please don't take all of the responsibility for his death! None of us are perfect! Just look at us three!'

Camilla kissed Charles on both cheeks, saying, 'Thank you for being so caring, and even though I am now married, if you feel like a change, please call me!' And she gave him her card whilst smiling and squeezing his right buttock.

As Charles opened the front door, he found a handsome man of about 30, with blond short hair and a moustache, staring at him.

'Is Mrs Brown in, I must speak urgently to her.'

Camilla smiled as she recognised the next guest. 'Why, Jules, what brings you here at such an hour? Oh, sorry, Charles Bishop, this is Julian Metals. He was a work colleague of Wills at Nuts and Bolts, and a good friend of mine. In fact, I spoke with Jules a few hours ago, and he gave me some good advice and courage about my predicament which convinced me to come and confess.'

Julian shook hands with Charles, then looked him up and down, smiling broadly. 'Oh, I can see why Willie liked you so!'

Charles said goodbye to Camilla, and watched her stride down the road like some mythical Greek Amazonian warrior. He was thinking some very bad thoughts. Charles sighed.

Julian cleared his throat, interrupting Charles' fantasy. 'Yes, she's a fine-looking woman with such a zest for life,' and he gave Charles a broad smile and a wink.

Charles, still looking at the disappearing goddess, replied, 'Oh, you were friends then?'

Julian nodded. 'Yes, we became very good friends. In fact, I was with her the last time that Camilla saw Willie alive.'

'Oh, you were the Jules she was talking about!'

Julian started crying. 'Yes, I'm not sure whether Willie was more upset with me rather than with Camilla. You see, we were very good friends as well. We loved our golf and other activities together so much!'

Charles couldn't help laughing, and after offering Julian his handkerchief, remarked, 'And I suppose one thing led—'

Julian wiping his eyes and blowing his nose interrupted, 'Led to another. You are so right. You know, you are such a sensitive man, I suppose you are happily married? I'm always available if you want, well, let's say, a shoulder to cry on, or some comforting!' With that Julian looked Charles up and down again, smiling, and gave another wink.

Charles felt very uncomfortable all of a sudden as he started imagining that Camilla's and Julian's lust for life could sometimes involve intimate relations with two others at the same time. A picture of Camilla, Julian, him, and one other, in one bed together formed in his mind.

Anne shouted from the living room, causing the picture to disappear, 'Charles, either let whoever is there in, or go outside, either way, close the blasted front door dearest sweetheart.'

Julian enquired, 'Please Charlie can I come in? I must confess!'

Charles shrugged. 'Why not? Let's get it all over and done with once and for all!'

He shouted into the lounge, 'Sally you have another visitor.'

He turned to Julian 'Be gentle! Up until a couple of hours ago Sally thought there were only three in her marriage, but tonight she has found out that there were actually more. Do you know whether there are any others she should know about?'

Julian shook his head. 'Not any that I'm aware of! Oh, by the way, was that Frankie I saw leaving your house earlier?'

Charles smiled. 'You mean Frank Beesley?'

'Yes, that's him! He and I are great friends! We love our art! Although these days he's been seeing a great deal of a woman called Anne. He met her through a mutual friend of theirs, named Christina, I think. Well, between you and me, Frankie says that this Anne, Christina Trout, Gerry, and, um, yes, and Camilla's larger-than-life sister, Samantha, play an unusual version of the card game, bridge, most Saturdays whilst their husbands play golf! He says they call it "Strip Bridge"! Just shows what goes on in London these days!' Julian smiled, winked at Charles, and continued. 'That Samantha certainly does have a zest for life!'

Charles sighed, and said, 'I don't believe it, Anne, eh? That's very interesting, illuminating and revealing! I understand perfectly now! I suppose in their case, one thing led to another!'

Jullian laughed, saying, 'Yes, that's one way of putting it! That's exactly what Frankie said, "It started off as contract bridge, but one thing led to another, and it ended up as contact bridge!" Oh, just a second, you don't mean you know this Anne?'

Charles nodded, confessing, 'Know her, and married to her!' Charles had a thought. *So that's why Anne has been so understanding about me and Sally! She feels guilty about her dirty little secret! Well, actually, thinking about it, it's a massive dirty secret! All these years she's been, oh well, best not to dwell on it!*

Julian had gone bright red. 'Oh, so sorry, if you didn't know! A bit of a shock then?'

'You could say that, Julian! Come and meet her! You'll find you have much in common, especially when it comes to art! However, from what you say, I don't think that your friendship with her will involve one thing leading to another!'

Charles closed the front door, and shouted into the lounge, 'Anne, more coffee dear, we'll all need it!'

Suddenly a thought came into his mind. *Just hold on a minute, Charlie! Didn't Katie Neugent say that she and Anne played bridge together? I wonder if, no surely not! But then again, based upon tonight's events, you just never know, Charlie Boy! Perhaps one thing led to another regarding those two as well! What a thought! I'm going to have nightmares tonight, that's if I ever get any sleep!*

Then he turned to Julian and whispered, 'I'd appreciate it if you would tell the complete story about Frank as well, including the bridge part! I think it's time for my wife to confess! It seems to me that I've led a relatively boring married life compared to others.

82

Although there were a few occasions when I was behind enemy lines in Belgium when, well, one thing led to another between me and some of the young female resistance fighters! Best if we keep quiet about those, Julian! Even my cat, Winston, has been sworn to secrecy!'

Printed in Great Britain
by Amazon